The Lie

Minerva Noiropp

Presentation by *BookLeaf Publishing*

Web: www.bookleafpub.com

E-mail: info@bookleafpub.com

ISBN: 9789395756693

First edition 2022

DEDICATION

God, without whose almight power I would not still be alive and on the path to thriving.

ACKNOWLEDGEMENT

All my enemies for providing me with excellent subject matter, both in observation of futile behaviour and the occasional insights of wisdom from said observation.

PREFACE

Start reading.

Enlightened

You were probably expecting some enlightened words.
Bad news, I would not even piss on you turds.
Is that a swear word, hypocrites, quick, judge me,
Through your covered, blind eye. How can you fools see?
All of your lies, I'm stalked by you liars.
Don't you see yet, I don't burn in your fires.
You can try, you can die, you can lie all you might.
You will never extinguish my pure soul's true light.
I know the rules. I've learned the truth.
I'm no longer hampered by the illusional booth.
Stalked by the Elite and their pet dogs, the Masons.
And by the masses of asses trying to earn their vacations.
I will stand strong, and I will remain firm.
Because one day Gods wrath with make each one of you squirm.

Soul Physics

Eyes closed; I connect.
Silent mind; introspect.
Sun covers the ground.
Illumination, in my head doth pound.
Brightness, lightness, spreads throughout.
Is this God's energy? No doubt.
Everything is God.
Some of it is fraud.
The Illuminati illusion,
To cause confusion.
It infiltrates.
It is never too late.
To block the noise,
Of the Devil's toys.
Back in the zone,
Smooth music from the phone.
My mind is blank,
As I zoom into planck.
It becomes clear,
And fills me with cheer,
As I delve into physics,
Of metaphysics.
Mass tells space time how to curve,
It bends reality, can we swerve?
Space time tells mass how to move.

This theory, how can I disprove?
I can't.
I shan't.
Souls live in eternity.
They have no mass. Do you see?
Jesus was more than a healer,
With souls he was a wheeler.
He understood.
Like we should,
The truth about sewing and reaping.
Does your soul do the creeping?
There are truths, that are spiritual,
That affect the physical.
Eternity and time,
Reaping of the crime,
Consequence of choice,
Right use of the voice.
Does my poem make sense?
Should you start in repentance?
I let the connection go.
I have much good news to sew.

Ayin 666

Let us start off with a little Hebrew,
Even if you are not inclined towards a Jew.
Eye is represented by the word Ayin.
This double speak language is no less than a sin.
Have you noticed that we all live in a lie,
That is purported by the Illuminati evil eye?
Have you picked up on the subtle gaslighting?
Of those who want to keep you mired in the
action of fighting.
Have you seen through the cracks of this world's
mental matrix?
Even if you are a member who is paid to play
tricks?
Let us disseminate a prominent number.
666: it is Carbon, could you lot play dumber?
If you want to add the numbers, well, look at
your tarot card.
It's the realm of deception and illusion. How is
that hard?
Forget about all your innuendos and fibs.
No, this next movement will not tickle your ribs.
What is a form of prison for a soul?
The Flesh. We are carbon. Enlightenment is the
goal.
The physical life is geared as a distraction.

To prevent us from putting our soul into action.
Our spirits have power. Oh, why can you not
see?
Why is speaking with God always left up to me?
These are demons, I say, controlling all our
external lives.
Their symbolism is how they work in their
hidden hives.
A liberated mind is an incredible danger.
When you have one, by all, you will be treated a
stranger.
Because you see past the veil, see through their
façade,
Of mere mortal fakes who try to convince you
they are God.
The pure soul has worth, it has power divine,
To divide and conquer the serpent bloodline.
A single pure soul is all that it takes,
To empty the world of the poisonous snakes.
The war is spiritual, it has been here a long time,
Good versus evil. Righteousness versus crime.
It takes a strong soul to stand firm and alone,
Deep within one must go through the process to
atone.
It shatters. It tears. It brings one to tears,
And washes one clean of all of one's fears.
On the material, they like to keep us all focused,
Like the plague that they are, so much worse
than a locust.

This distraction keeps us from our soul's
evolution.
In our minds, it keeps spirit so full of pollution.
Take one step, take two, please start on that path.
You do not have to be smart to work out the
math.
It is for you, not for me, that I write these words
now.
Will you read them and ignore me any old how?
I can not save you, nor liberate you free.
It is up to you, how you want to be.
The consequence is you will have to be reborn,
In a future where Human Rights have all been
shorn.
The pattern has emerge. They step on all of us,
Like an unstoppable, out of control,
broken-braked bus.
Open your eyes, observe, and see.
You never, not ever, have to side with me.

Individual Who Is Targeted

I am an individual who is targeted.
This shit has messed me bad in my head.
It is an evil campaign, much like the Stasi.
Each stalker is equivalent to a reborn Nazi.
It started at birth. No escaping that fact.
My conscienceless family entered into demonic
a pact.
This op is run by Freemasons and Illuminati,
The military and police are part of that family.
I am a good-hearted woman, not doing wrong.
These terrorists harass me. They are weak and
not strong.
They plot how to hurt me, to drive me insane.
Your damn right if you think that I think they're
a pain.
They try to control my mind, to force me onto
my knees.
These criminals are nothing better than
cancerous disease.
They've stolen, they lied both to me and about.
I've caught them in action, of this there's no
doubt.
They've run a line past me, that I deserve this.
As an excuse to try to deny me of bliss.
I changed my whole self, within to without.

Found out that I have a touch of spiritual clout.
From sin to righteousness and balanced my
Karma.
I really don't give two hoots about any false
Dharma.
I found out what they said was a self-serving lie,
In their attempt to try and get me to die.
Their evil has shoved me onto a glorious path,
Where in God's almighty energy I take a
spiritual bath.
His light will illume, outside and in.
Following God's law is never a sin.

The Eye

I am stalked, hounded, followed by the eye,
Living in an Illuminati, Freemason, gang
stalking lie.
The Devil, the eye, that is lacking a soul,
A bottomless devourer that can never fill its
hole.
Follows me in my house, it follows me every
day,
Please understand, you bastards, I will not obey!
No privacy, I am spied upon, never left alone,
By a bunch of smooth talkers faking being on
the phone.
Street theatre, bad actors, my goodness, what a
joke.
I can see through their BS. No fire, but lots of
smoke.
And the countless things that they want me to
attach to,
I could not care less. It is all a lie. It is not true.
The stupidity is that these fools think I should
respond.
Oh, you bloody idiots, you slaves, you have all
been conned.
The mindless masses, obeying without thought.

Should you use your mind? I know that I ought.
It is a farce, all these people doing their things,
An act they put on around me. Their conscience,
does it not sting?
Their falsehood tastes in the mouth, like a dead
fire's ash.
Their behaviour nothing better than a third
graders trash.
It degrades, these monsters, stalkers, living
nightmare,
If this was each of you, my oh my, you would
yell "Not fair!"
But it is not you, it is me.
You ignore my humanity.
You do not see who I am,
Because you are all so full of your own scam.
You forgot I am a person, I bleed the same as
each one of you.
I have emotions, feelings, hopes and dreams, all
of this is true.
What will it take, to get you to recognise me and
leave me to myself?
What needs to happen to make your asinine
ways end up on a shelf?
I have the right to live and have a fullness of
life,
Without your interference or you bringing me
your strife.
If you people would just give me half a chance,

You would see how I can help others in this life
learn how to dance.
Will my words ever make on the masses an
impact?
Or will these deadened souls spend eternity in a
red-hot tract?
The consequence to your stalking me is more far
reaching than you know,
The Devil has you in his vice, you stalkers are
naught but the Devil's ho.
Why am I the wisest one, the person who sees
past the illusion?
Is this Biblical and truly the Devil's confusion?
Is this all written, and I'm playing a specific
part?
Of one of God's elect; a saint who is close to his
heart?
To believe this is so dangerous, but throughout
ancient history,
The signs line up, it is all there, words written
about those who are not me.
I have so much in common with them. Were
they all targeted too?
How much of history is a lie and how much of it
true?
Round and round in my head, thoughts chased
from head to tail.
Is it in a cup, or is it me, am I the Holy Grail?

One thing that I know for sure is I will stand
firm to the end,
And I will never trust another person to ever
consider them a friend.

The Wrong End of Black Ops

I would not back the blue,
Even if you paid me to.
I would not support the cops,
Because of their criminal black ops.
Military are guilty too,
Uniform black, green, red, white or blue.
I have done nothing wrong,
All I want is to sing a song.
The bastards are stalking me,
And everyone is too blind to see.
Instead, they all join to oppress,
To try and give me a lot of stress.
But I am not in the dark,
And this game is not a lark.
Where are my Human Rights?
Why in cruelty must you all delights?
Why am I unlike most?
Am I a vessel or a host?
I am on a path,
I do not want God's wrath.
I follow Karmic law.
Your own conclusion you must draw.
I obey his word.
My soul is quickened and it is stirred.
Why can I elevate my mind?

Why, even now, am I so kind?
Liberation is key.
It is what is meant for me.

Psyops – Social Media Branch

Twitter, Facebook, Instagram.
Look at the lies, it is all a sham.
Look at the Devil's tares,
They are everywhere.
Promoting all of their fake,
In the service of the snake.
It was meant to be a tool,
However, I am not a fool.
The purpose; insidious.
The truth; hideous.
It was never meant for us.
It is to spread the Elite mind virus.
Evil words flow like honey.
From those who sold souls for dollop of money.
What has happened to the truth?
Why must I always play the sleuth?
Their words have no meaning.
I ponder and try to get a gleaning.
Idiots talking tit for tat,
In some backwards online chit chat.
Social Media is a huge psyop.
A militarised psychological op.
To spread the disinformation.
That's right! It is the Freemasons.

The best way to control the people,
Is to divide under the steeple.
As for individuals who are targets,
They use it to hound them with their human
pets.
To keep one from grasping the big picture,
And try to bind them in a stricture.
But words have very little power,
Even when delivered with a glower,
Against an illuminated mind,
Who is not part of the Elite grind.

Devilish Dreams

Desperate today, aren't you mister Devil?
You dance in my dreams, and in your evil you
revel.
It has been constant, this dreamscape
manipulation,
Trying to lower me to beneath my current
spiritual station.
First you try with a deal that your goons will not
back up.
Then you try to force me to sin with an evil,
poisoned cup.
That doesn't work, so you come at me with
force,
Trying to get into me, trying upon me to sin
enforce.
And how did that go for you, as I called in my
angelic crew?
For every black you tried to beat me they did
beat you blue.
You've tried to kill me in waking life.
You've brought me endless amounts of strife.
You try to murder me in my dreams,
Where nothing is as ever as it seems.
Hear me loud now and hear me clear.

With my body, mind, and soul thou shalt not
interfere.
I can deal with your war for every single day
and night,
Of my life, because I'd rather keep my Karma
clean and in the right.
I don't want to engage in immorality.
It would affect my peaceful afterlife immortality.
United with God, we will stand, and together we
will win.
Against an evil, immoral nation in forever
bondage to your sin.

Agenda 2070

Let me not be too vague,
Expect in 2070 a return of the Black Plague.
These Freemasons and the Elite,
Understand astrology. Is not that neat?
Past, present, future, in a linear line,
It is all written in the stars. Is not that divine?
Research history. Study an astrology chart.
Prepare for the future. Is not that smart?
Covid was a warm-up, it was just a hint.
It wasn't much more than a joke of a stint.
No, it was not fun. It was not very funny.
It is amazing what people will do for a small
sum of money.
Everyone was happy to trample on my rights.
Everyone was pleased, it brought them such
delight.
Their rights got trampled, too. And they will be
in the future.
Won't be any nurses left with a needle or a
suture.
Between the gang stalking, climate change, and
various a crisis,
There won't be a doctor left to deal with
childrens' encephalitis.

It is karma; the bottom line.
These words are your sign.
Are you prepared to reap the consequences of
what you sew?
Or will you ignore the call to action and
continue to say no?
Some behaviour has got to end if humanity is to
survive,
The 99% are destined not to even thrive.
Time is catching up. Deeds done need to be in
balance.
Are you going to err, or on my words will you
take a chance?

Won in the Mind

The battle is won in the mind,
In the world of the unreal.
Every day I seek, search, and find,
My life is so surreal.

The war in heaven is won.
It is just playing out here.
The battles are not so fun,
Having to deal with goons who interfere.

I am on the winning streak now.
I finally learned the formula.
I will claim victory any old how.
No longer MK Ultra.

Deprogrammed and released the control.
No one can manipulate me.
I will evolve my soul.
You lot will all watch and see.

Everywhere

Look at the matrix,
And read the rhyme,
Observe as they play tricks,
Watch them neck deep in their crimes.

It is in the brand names,
And colours too.
I do not play games,
Do you love blue?

It is in your medication,
It is in your food,
It is in your PlayStation,
To alter your mood.

Nothing is chance.
It is written in a script.
It is not happenstance.
It will lead you to the crypt.

You are the one who is under control.
I remain free.
You have murdered your soul.
Enlighten me.

You are their pet.
I am a free agent.
You cannot escape their net,
Without the reagent.

Now what would you do?
To become like me?
You would choose not to screw,
For eternity.

The Karma game,
That they have you play,
Is a trap all the same,
Yet, fool, you obey.

You reincarnate.
I have forever peace.
That you will hate,
For your life you decease.

Hex

You spy.
You sly.
You lie.
You cry.

You try.
You fly.
You sky.
You high.

You scry.
You shy.
You guy.
You fry.

You sigh.
You why?
You eye.
…

No Honey, Not You.

See, I can play with words too,
Just like the rest of you.
But my intent is not the same,
As you predators' evil game.
I am proving a point.
Don't get your noses out of joint.
That me, you people shall not rule.
For I am not paid to be a fool.
My Karma, I will not destroy.
Because love of the Lord doth bring me joy.
I obey my God,
For he is not a fraud.
God is not a farce,
Each word is part of a parse.
Do you people yet understand?
I am not yours to ever command.
My soul purpose is much higher,
Than doing deeds for all you liars.
Karma is very real,
But I doubt my words you feel.
For your energy is fake,
You vile offspring of the snake.
You are all so blind and deaf,
It will lead you all to eternal death.
Give me life any day,

I have no karma left to pay.
Eternal peace is for me,
It is my choice. So, mote it be.

Destruction

Look at the fake news,
It just makes me want to spew.
Where are the real facts?
Are they so scared they might redact?
Why such pointless stories?
Lots of bs, and somewhat gory.
It is an attack upon the mind.
Answers I seek but never find.
It is a form of control,
Designed to covertly destroy your soul.
This entire world is a battleground.
Demons upon humans forever pound.
But it is so subtle,
Evil forces on the scuttle.
I am the only one who seems to see,
Their evil movement beneath the tree.
Where are the good guys?
To fight the Lord of the Flies?
We need back up of the good.
We need the angels from the wood.
The world is going down the tube.
Most to be imprisoned in the cube,
Through addictions and their jobs.
External attachments I must fob.
I care no longer for the masses.

They forgot to cover their asses.
They have treated me so bad.
I could not care less if they are sad.
I will look after me,
And climb my way up the eternal tree.
For that is my salvation,
From a rapidly dying nation.
I used to feel so much,
And they used it against me, it was my crutch.
I used to care for all the people.
Now I care not for all the sheeple.
They destroyed my love for them.
They are now nothing more than stale phlegm.
When you abuse a good person,
Blame yourselves, your own lives you've chosen
to worsen.
Because that person will walk away,
And make the choice to never play.
Never lose a persons' loyalty,
It is worth more than royalty.
But the damage has been done.
And in the end, this war I've won.

Saint

I'm on the path of being a saint.
Does that make you all feel faint?
By your own words, you all are liars,
Who start unnecessary fires.
That means you all engage in arson,
In the end it is you all who are the con,
In eternity,
Because of your paternity,
As you are all children of Satan,
Who are as sincere as a spray tan.
You will never win against me,
Because I have divinity,
From without and within.
This is how the war I win.
The games of the mentally ill,
Who are in bondage to the Devil,
Have already lost,
It is your own soul it has cost.
Our spirit lasts forever,
Destroying it is never clever.
Because of it you all will suffer.
There is no way you can defer.
When you realise your debt,
You've sold yourselves into bondage as a pet.
Why do I waste my breath,
On those who choose to worship death?

The End of an Evil Cycle

Your program is coming to end,
You people who are not my friend.
Your interference in my life,
Of your wish to cause me strife,
Will be brought to a close.
That's right, your dead, all of you pet ho's.
It was never me. It always was you creeps,
It will be your tears shed, and over your children
you will weep.
Your evil is exiting my realm.
I am the one standing at my helm.
No more control of my mind.
If you want, it is you who grind.
I am not sure when or how.
At the time it will be now.
God is sending intervention.
These words are no light mention.
Whether you like it or not.
Become conscious you mindless bots.
I don't care if you believe,
As it will be you who will leave,
Me alone.
You will all atone,
For the evil you have done,

Because I am my own number one.
Everyone will pay their karmic debt,
You sick freaks who tried to make me your pet.
I am an individual sovereign,
My mind is not in a chain.
I think for myself.
Put your ego on a shelf.
You will learn to give me birth,
Because of my infinitesimal spiritual worth.
In the end you will wish you had made the deal.
Because I am a gal who keeps it real.

Temporality

The flesh is temporary. The soul is eternal.
I do what I need to do to keep me from the
infernal.
I discovered the value of what the Bible does
say.
I learned to differentiate from the false Christian
heresy.
I do not give a damn about my physical enemy.
It boils down to this in life, it is either them or
me.
My enemy has sold their soul, they are in
bondage to the eye.
Not me. No deal there. Not a word out of me
will lie.
I will not give up my inherent soul spiritual
worth.
I have an abundance of energy. Within there is
no dearth.
If I could be given a dollar value of my soul.
Even thousand-dollar bills could not fill up a ten
by ten metre hole.
Instead, a soul's value is not demonstrated
through dollar signs.
One can see it in how they live their life, in how
they obey God's grand design.

I make an active choice to follow my Lord God
of all.
To save myself from an unprecipitated fall.
It does not matter who or what is against my life.
It is irrelevant what moron brings me strife.
Greater within me is the eternal might God.
Than the Devil who is in the world; the
temporary fraud.

Hell

It is not what you think.
The souls from it do stink.
It is not part of endlessness.
It is trapped in time, hell yes.
Hell, it's a place.
A place with no grace.
It is real,
And surreal.
It is next to, within and overlaps,
The world we live in. It is a trap.
There is no rest for the wicked.
Who chose to act like a dickhead.
There is no escape for evil souls.
A trap in time, it swallows you whole.
It is terrifying,
A fate worse than dying.
A curse of existence.
Why I am at repentance.
It is not where I will end up,
Even if all I have in life is an empty cup.
Because my spirit runneth over.
Will a soul filled to the brim with clover.
I have glimpsed eternal from without.
It is my destination, no doubt.
Align my behavious with the outcome.

A strategy of wisdom, not dumb.
As for each and every fool,
Who did not attend spiritual school.
You will reap as you each sew.
It is your decision on where you go.

Guarded

I don't know what, do I have a shield?
You masses of asses could not defeat me on the
field.
I don't know what, do I have a guard?
Is that the reasons your attacks fail so hard?
I don't know what, do I have an angel?
I will never be brought down into your strange
hell.
I don't know what, is it God with me?
I can outride any storm on the sea.
I don't know what, is that Jesus within?
That gives me the strength to rebuke every sin.
I don't know what, is the Holy Spirit here?
I keep my souls allies so close and so near.
An invisible team, I am so guarded.
Splinter your army and leave all of you sharded.

Truth

It gets easier every single day,
To ignore you creeps and refuse to obey.
Because the power that I serve.
Is higher than you, my loyalty you don't
deserve.
You treated me bad. You destroyed my life.
You sent your slaves towards me and brought
me nothing but strife.
God stepped in and said no more.
Gaid said to me, you are not one of their whores.
You know what? God is right.
He has given me the strength to win this unholy
fight.
We don't have a deal and we never will.
I don't sign up with terrorists of the Devil.

The End

Game over, done and dusted.
All you liars, just been busted.
Lots of talk and no movement.
You timewasters can all get bent.
We could have had it good, if you had made the deal.
I'm a business gal, I like to keep it real.
I stand my ground. I won't back off.
Cover your mouth, freaks, when you cough.
I guess you'll enjoy your defeat.
So much for you all being elite.
All I see is a bunch of fakes.
In eternal bondage to an evil snake.
He is your dad, he isn't mine.
I belong to God. Is that not divine?
Have you people not cottoned on?
I'm a free agent. I am not a con.
I guess you spy but you don't observe.
Wait till its your turn to get a Karmic serve.
The wheel it turns, and it will turn around.
Those on top will need to go to ground.
Why on earth would people want to pay?
When with God's holy chosen you should not play.
I will not give up my salvation.

Even in the face of a starving nation.
Mark my words and here me clear,
You sick, creepy perverts who interfere.
God has declared this war is won.
And with you losers my time is done.
Whether you like how this story ends.
You lying, cursed people, we will never be
friends.

www.ingramcontent.com/pod-product-compliance
Lightning Source LLC
LaVergne TN
LVHW010825200726
843508LV00012B/2500